MANY OF THE WORDS WE US
IN ENGLISH COME FROM TH
SPOKEN BY ANCIENT ROMAN
WORDS YOU WILL ALREADY KN
ANIMAL, CIRCUS, HORROR, ACTOR...

TOUGH TIMES™

THE ANCIENT ROMAN WAY OF LIFE WAS ONLY POSSIBLE BECAUSE THEY HAD SLAVES, PEOPLE WHO HAVE HAD THEIR FREEDOM TAKEN FROM THEM.

# A KID'S LIFE IN ANCIENT ROME

## GROWING UP IN ANCIENT ROME

THE AUTHOR OF **A KID'S LIFE IN ANCIENT ROME** IS ROGER CANAVAN, AN AWARD-WINNING AUTHOR OF SCIENCE BOOKS AND OTHER INFORMATION BOOKS FOR CHILDREN.

THE ARTIST IS DAVID ANTRAM. HE STUDIED AT EASTBOURNE COLLEGE OF ART AND WORKED IN ADVERTISING BEFORE BECOMING A FULL-TIME ILLUSTRATOR.

PUBLISHED IN GREAT BRITAIN IN MMXIX BY
BOOK HOUSE, AN IMPRINT OF
THE SALARIYA BOOK COMPANY LTD
25 MARLBOROUGH PLACE, BRIGHTON BN1 1UB
WWW.SALARIYA.COM

ISBN: 978-1-912537-56-3

1 3 5 7 9 8 6 4 2

A CIP CATALOGUE RECORD FOR THIS BOOK IS AVAILABLE FROM THE BRITISH LIBRARY.
PRINTED AND BOUND IN CHINA.

# TOUGH TIMES™

Boys' Names:
Albus (Bright)
Augustus (Great)

Girls' Names:
Flavia (Yellow hair)
Luciana (Light)

# A KID'S LIFE IN ANCIENT ROME

## GROWING UP IN ANCIENT ROME

The text is written by
**ROGER CANAVAN**
And the illustrations are by
**DAVID ANTRAM**

This book is
Published by
Book House

# CONTENTS

PAGES 18 AND 19 ARE ABOUT THE SIZE OF THE ROMAN EMPIRE AND HOW IT DEFENDED ITSELF.

PAGES 20 AND 21 ARE ABOUT WHAT ROMAN CHILDREN WERE TAUGHT AT SCHOOL.

PAGES 22 AND 23 ARE ABOUT THE DANGERS AND DELIGHTS TO BE FOUND IN THE CITY OF ROME.
PAGES 24 AND 25 ARE ABOUT THE ROMAN GODS AND HOW THEY WERE WORSHIPPED.
PAGES 28 AND 29 ARE ABOUT WHAT ROMANS GOT UP TO IN THE TOWN OF POMPEII.

PAGES 26 AND 27 ARE ABOUT HOW ROMANS SPENT A WORKING DAY.
PAGES 30 AND 31 ARE THE GLOSSARY AND PAGE 32 IS THE INDEX.

# INTRODUCTION

By the time that Rome became the heart of its empire it was the largest and most powerful city on Earth. Most Romans were either hard-working craftsmen or slaves, but the richest Romans were elite patricians who led lives of luxury. Their children would grow up to lead Rome's famous armies or become powerful political figures in Roman society.

WHAT WILL I DO WHEN I GROW UP? DEFEAT ROME'S ENEMIES ON THE BATTLEFIELD... OR BE A POWERFUL POLITICIAN AT HOME? I HAVEN'T DECIDED YET!

## INSIDE KNOWLEDGE

### PLEBEIANS

These Romans were not as privileged or wealthy as the patricians, but they had full rights as citizens. The plebeians owned small farms and lived in small villas around the cities. Being full citizens meant that they could sometimes play a part in local government.

### FACT

Although a patrician child would have slaves, he still lived in a world of strict regulations, rules, laws and customs – and they provided plenty of chances for a child to get into big trouble.

## MAP OF THE ROMAN EMPIRE

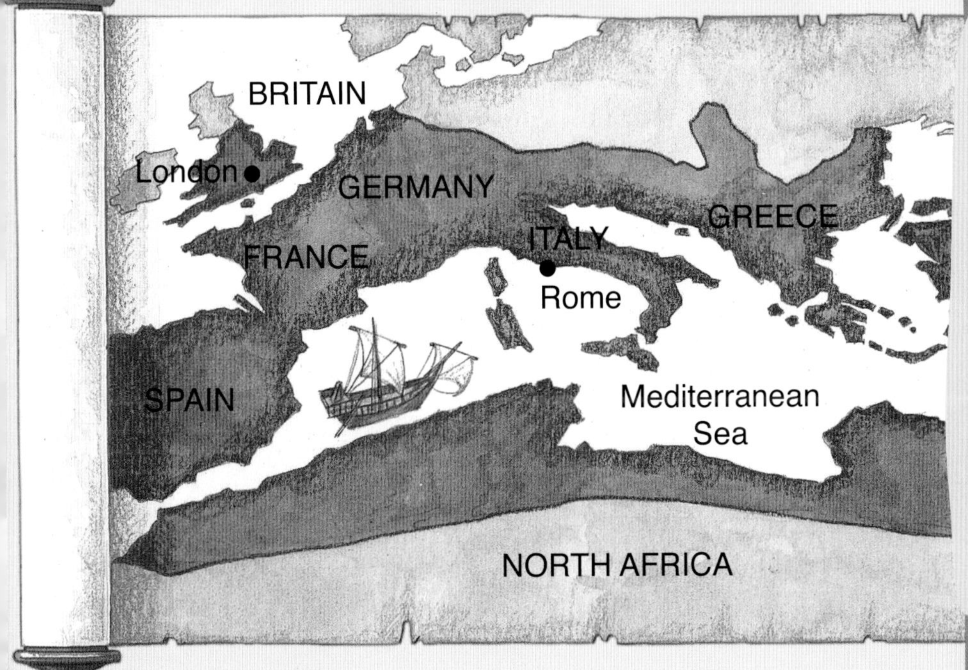


# BAD THINGS HAPPEN

### FACT

Owners would free slaves that had outlived their use by being too old to work. The owner wouldn't then have to look after these slaves in their old age. Slaves who acted as nannies would sometimes be freed once they were no longer needed by their owner's children.

### HEAVEN OR HELL?

Patrician marriages were usually decided by the fathers of the bride and groom. The young couple had little say in who would become their husband or wife. Instead, the marriage linked two families to preserve wealth or power. The bride's family would provide a dowry, or gift of money, to help run the household.

### FACT

Plebeians struggled for many years against the rule of Rome's patricians. Sometimes, in protest, they would leave the city, or go on strike, or refuse to fight in the army. They finally gained the same legal rights, allowing them to hold political office and even marry patricians.

# WHO DO YOU THINK YOU ARE?

My life in Rome isn't so hard, but then... I'm a patrician, one of the wealthiest and richest Romans. Our slaves and servants are here to help, and to do all the hard work of keeping the household spick and span. After all, someone has to buy our food and cook it, mend clothes and make sure there is fuel for our fires. I suppose our slaves might not think that their lives are so easy...

MY COUSIN IS GETTING MARRIED NEXT MONTH. SHE JUST TURNED TWELVE, AND THE BOY SHE'S MARRYING IS FOURTEEN.

## INSIDE KNOWLEDGE

### THE MAIN MAN

The man of the house, or paterfamilias ('father of the family'), had full legal control over everyone who lived there. That really did mean everyone, including his wife, his children and all his servants and slaves.

### MISTRESS OF THE HOUSE

A wealthy woman would be a citizen of Rome but could not vote or go into politics. Although her husband had legal control over everything – and everyone – in the household, she would usually make sure that everything ran smoothly. But, of course, her slaves helped her to dress and get her hair looking just right.

# BAD THINGS HAPPEN

## ROMAN SLAVES

A wealthy family would have many slaves. The rich needed lots of help to live in luxury, and that's where slaves came in. Some slaves would fetch high prices if they had a special skill, like being able to prepare a feast or tame a horse.

## FREE AT LAST

An owner would sometimes reward a slave by granting him his freedom. Some slaves managed to scrape together the money to buy their freedom. These 'freedmen' and 'freedwomen' often became craftsmen and traders. Others became servants to rich people or took jobs working for the government.

## FACT

Not every slave was stuck doing hard or menial work. Sometimes book-keepers and teachers – and even some doctors – were slaves in ancient Rome.

# INSIDE KNOWLEDGE

## NAMING DAYS

Babies weren't given names until they were just over a week old. That's because so many babies died in the first days of life. Girls were named when they were eight days old, and boys when they were nine days old. Families and friends would present gifts and a sacrifice would also be made to the gods.

## FACT

A boy born to a wealthy family would receive a special locket called a bulla on his naming day. The bulla would protect him from evil, and he would wear it until he became a man.

# ENTERING THE WORLD

My father's power was obvious as soon as I was born. The midwife laid me, a newborn baby, on the ground at my father's feet. By picking me up, my father was signalling that I would be kept. A baby born with a disability, or who is unwanted because the family already has too many children, or because she is a girl, will be left outside in a public place.

MY NAME IS MARCUS AURELIUS ANTONINUS. MY PARENTS CHOSE MY FIRST NAME, MARCUS. MY MIDDLE NAME, AURELIUS, HONOURS MY CLAN AND ANTONINUS IS THE NAME OF THE FAMILY THAT ADOPTED ME.

# BAD THINGS HAPPEN

## PAINFUL ARRIVAL

Childbirth was dangerous, even for the wealthiest of Romans. Both mother and baby were often lucky to survive the ordeal. Bleeding and infection were the biggest risks. The birth itself was an 'all woman' affair. A midwife would be in charge, with female family members helping her and looking after the newborn child.

### FACT

Roman emperors often adopted a favourite boy to succeed them as emperor. Marcus Aurelius became Roman emperor in AD 161. He had been adopted by Emperor Hadrian.

### FACT

Some skilled midwives delivered babies 'part time' while working on other jobs. One Roman wine-shop owner left her shop to deliver a neighbour's baby. She returned, washed her hands and continued serving her customers.

# CHILDHOOD

Childhood in Rome is divided into clearly defined stages. Boys and girls stay at home until the age of seven. Parents, grandparents, older brothers and sisters and slaves look after us. Young children like me are often spoiled, but we also have to learn about the responsibilities that we'll have in later life.

I GUESS I SHOULD ENJOY MYSELF WHILST I CAN, BECAUSE IT WON'T ALL BE FUN IN THE FUTURE.

## INSIDE KNOWLEDGE

### FIRST BIRTHDAY

Many babies died either at birth or in their first year. Funerals for infants were common, even among the wealthy. That was why achieving a first birthday (called an anniculus) was a cause for real celebration.

### FACT

Apart from reaching an important milestone, a one-year-old boy could become a Roman citizen (girls, and women, could only have limited citizenship).

### FACT

Children would get increased freedom, and responsibilities, as they approached their coming of age (about 12 for girls, 15 for boys).

## FACT

Many patrician boys attended a gymnasium during the day. There they practised sports like wrestling, but they also learned about how to be good Roman citizens when they were older.

# BAD THINGS HAPPEN

## OUT AND ABOUT

Before the age of seven, boys and girls were mostly kept inside the house. As boys grew older, they were allowed to go out and about far more freely. These 'escapes' from home offered excitement, but also the risk of robbery, disease... or simply getting lost in the world's largest city.

## SLAVE PLAYMATES

Many wealthy children became friends with the family's slave children, who were often the first people of a similar age that they knew. But these friendships often broke up suddenly if the slave child was sold. Happy relationships could disappear overnight.

## INSIDE KNOWLEDGE

### THE TABLINUM

The atrium was an important formal space in a Roman house, but beyond it was a room where the master's 'top secret' business was conducted. It was known as the tablinum, and it looked out onto the gardens or courtyard behind the house. The master's most important possessions would be stored in a chest in the tablinum.

### FACT

A wealthy family home would have a peristyle, or porch, running around a courtyard behind the tablinum. Columns lined this cool, shady area where people could admire the gardens and courtyard fountains as they strolled.

# HOME, SWEET HOME?

The heart of our Roman house is the atrium, an open central court with expensive rugs and statues. The atrium is a public, formal room where the paterfamilias (the male head of the household) receives guests or meets clients. Other rooms, each with its own special purpose, lead to or from the atrium and out into a courtyard.

MY FATHER ALWAYS KEEPS HIS CLIENTS WAITING IN THE ATRIUM FOR AS LONG AS POSSIBLE BEFORE MEETING THEM. IT GIVES THEM TIME TO BE IMPRESSED BY ALL THE WORKS OF ART THAT MY FATHER HAS ON DISPLAY SO THEY SEE HOW IMPORTANT HE IS.

## FACT

The ceiling of the atrium had a square opening called the compluvium to let rain through. It collected in a sunken pool below and slowly filtered through to a basin in the cool, dark chamber below. It provided the household's supply of fresh water.

# BAD THINGS HAPPEN

## CAVE CANEM

Keeping a fierce dog to warn intruders off isn't a new idea. Guard dogs protected many Roman homes. A warning of 'Cave Canem' (Beware of the Dog) often featured in mosaics by the threshold of a home. It definitely wasn't a good idea to anger a fierce dog.

## BLOCKS OF FLATS

Poorer Romans lived in crowded blocks of flats called insulae. In many ways, these were like modern blocks of flats, and were often seven or eight storeys high. Rome had as many as 44,000 insulae during the Imperial period.

# FANCY SOME ROAST PEACOCK?

Rich and poor Romans alike eat bread, cheese, olive oil and many fruits. But, of course, food for the wealthy can be quite different, especially when we are trying to impress guests. The menu at a formal banquet can include roast peacock, wild boar stuffed with live birds and even mice rolled in honey and poppy seeds. My family eat lying down on comfortable sofas, while slaves cut up our food and hand it to us.

I DARED MY BROTHER TO DRINK A WHOLE MUGFUL OF GARUM IN ONE GO. HE ONLY GOT HALFWAY THROUGH AND RAN OFF TO BE SICK!

## INSIDE KNOWLEDGE

### EARLY BREAKFAST

The Roman breakfast was eaten early, just after sunrise. Bleary-eyed family members would have salted bread, milk, dried fruit and maybe a bit of meat and cheese. Romans had no sugar, so they would sweeten food with honey. Slaves cut up and served the food to their masters.

### ROMAN KETCHUP

Just like children today, young Romans liked to smother their food with their favourite sauce. Ketchup didn't exist – they liked a thick, salty liquid called garum. This strong-tasting sauce was made of fish guts and it was really, really smelly.

# BAD THINGS HAPPEN

## LOCAL BAKERIES

Most poor families had no kitchen, so children would take food to a bakery to be cooked. All children on 'food delivery' duty hoped that the queue at the bakery was short. Otherwise, it meant returning to hungry parents that were furious to have been kept waiting for their dinner.

### FACT

As bread was an important part of the diet in ancient Rome, the poor were given loaves to stop them from rioting. Emperors promised 'bread and circuses' (food and entertainment) to the poor to keep them satisfied and under control.

### FACT

At banquets and special occasions some foods were meant to be seen as much as eaten. Birds' wings added to a roast hare made it look like a flying horse or a roast suckling pig might be served with an apple in its mouth as though it was eating it.

# INSIDE KNOWLEDGE

## CORNERS OF THE EMPIRE

Romans were surrounded by aspects of their far-reaching empire. Elephants and hippos from Africa, olives from Spain and woollen cloaks from Britain were all common sights. Even more striking was the sight of dark-skinned Africans or blond Germans in the ranks of a Roman legion. All were part of the great empire.

## FACT

Roman legions could march more than 30 kilometres (18 miles) a day. Most of the marching took place over only three hours, with soldiers carrying more than 20 kilograms (44 pounds) of equipment and weapons.

# HOW BIG IS THE EMPIRE?

Rome is the centre of our empire and the largest city in the world. About a million people live here. The Roman Empire was built and maintained on military strength. A wealthy young Roman boy like me might grow up to lead one of the famous Roman legions into far-flung places like Egypt, Spain... or Britain.

MY UNCLE FOUGHT IN BRITAIN, AND HE SAID THE WARRIORS ARE TERRIFYING. THEY WEAR NO ARMOUR AND PAINT THEIR BODIES BLUE. IT MUST BE TERRIFYING TO SEE THEM CHARGING TOWARDS YOU, SCREAMING AT THE TOP OF THEIR LUNGS.

### FACT

Many people from conquered lands were brought back to Rome to start new lives as slaves. It would have been a sad sight to see their hopeless procession through the capital.

# BAD THINGS HAPPEN

## PREPARE FOR BATTLE

Thoughts of war were always present, even for wealthy families. The empire was founded on its battles, and Rome's soldiers needed to take on enemies from all sides. Boys learned early on that courage and self-reliance were prized values. A patrician father would train his son to defend himself in battle.

### FACT

Fathers often took their sons to watch violent boxing matches, to teach them the best way to fight. Boxers fought either bare-handed or with leather straps wrapped around their knuckles. Knockouts were very common, especially if a boxer hid a metal bar under the leather straps.

# TIME FOR SCHOOL?

Sons of wealthy families like me are educated to be future Roman leaders. Formal training begins at the age of seven, when boys are taught at schools run by stern (and often Greek) teachers. Discipline is strict. Daydreaming, arriving late or repeatedly getting answers wrong can lead to serious trouble.

NO ONE WARNED ME HOW LONG MY SCHOOL DAY WOULD BE. I START AT SUNRISE, HAVE A SHORT LUNCH (BUT NO NAP!) AND DON'T GO HOME UNTIL SUNSET.

## INSIDE KNOWLEDGE

### NOISY SURROUNDINGS

Imagine trying to concentrate in a school that's separated from a busy street just by a thin curtain – and sometimes not even that! A Roman school rarely had its own building, or even a room with four walls. It was right in the heart of the city, with all the hustle and bustle that goes on each day.

### FACT

Roman kids used tablets at school! Pupils scratched their sums and writing onto wax tablets. These could be rubbed off easily if mistakes were made or in preparation for the next lesson.

## FACT

Boys went to school seven days a week, with no break for weekends. But they didn't go to school on every eighth (market) day, or the hundred or so religious holidays or for three months in summer.

# BAD THINGS HAPPEN

## PUNISHMENT

Schoolboys tried their hardest to avoid getting into trouble, because things could get very tough if they did. Pupils could be punished for arriving late for school, misbehaving, or failing to prepare for their lessons. Caning was the usual punishment, but a harsh teacher might get slaves to hold down a boy while he was whipped.

## FACT

Roman schoolboys ways are predictably familiar – like writing in the wrong place. The wall of an ancient Roman schoolroom has the phrase 'Socrates taedium est' (Socrates is boring) scrawled in a child's handwriting. Some things never change.

# INSIDE KNOWLEDGE

## THE COLOSSEUM

The Colosseum was the scene of thrilling – and frightening – battles between gladiators, animals, and sometimes a mixture of men and animals fighting to the death. The spectacle was unforgettable and often terrifying. Emperors sometimes punished Romans by cancelling popular games at the Colosseum.

## FACT

Chariot racing was almost as dangerous as gladiator battles in the Colosseum. Drivers were often seriously injured, or even killed, in crashes during races.

# HOW SAFE IS THE CITY?

Rome is full of exciting places to visit, such as the magnificent Forum, lofty temples, sports arenas and viewpoints overlooking valleys and distant mountains. But it is also a place of mystery and even a little fear. Thieves lurk in dark alleys. Guard dogs are waiting to pounce. And just beyond the city walls are the catacombs, a maze of caves where many Romans are buried that extend deep underground.

WHOSE IDEA WAS IT TO EXPLORE THESE CATACOMBS? I'VE HEARD THAT PEOPLE GET LOST EXPLORING THEM... AND NEVER COME OUT. WHO KNOWS THE QUICKEST WAY OUT OF HERE?

# BAD THINGS HAPPEN

## PUBLIC MEANS PUBLIC

Public toilets really were public. You didn't enter a private cubicle and lock the door before sitting down. Instead, you had to sit on one of the holes on a long stone bench, alongside about ten other people. Water rushing beneath the bench would 'flush' anything away. You wouldn't want to get caught short or you'd need to use one of these cold, smelly toilets!

### FACT

A giant sun shade could be rolled out to protect spectators in the Colosseum. Bakeries and drinks stalls made sure that people had enough to eat and drink at the games.

### FACT

Romans did not have toilet paper. Instead, a Roman would use a spongia, a sea sponge attached to a long stick. The spongia was shared by everyone and rinsed in the running water below the toilet.

# THE GODS

In ancient Rome, religion is important and complicated. We worship thousands of gods, and believe that everything, including trees, mountains, houses and rivers has a guardian spirit to watch over it. As an aristocratic boy, I need to learn how, when and where to honour these gods because one day, like my father, I will lead my own family in worship of the gods.

AT MY FIRST SACRIFICE, I WAS LOOKING FORWARD TO SOME TASTY COOKED MEAT AFTERWARDS. JUST MY LUCK - THEY WERE SACRIFICING A BROWN DOG, TO CELEBRATE THE 'DOG DAYS' OF SUMMER. YUCK!

## INSIDE KNOWLEDGE

### ANIMAL SACRIFICE

Many Roman celebrations and ceremonies involved animal sacrifices. These were a way of communicating with gods, heroes and other divine beings. A range of animals were used for sacrifice, including cattle, sheep, pigs, chickens and even dogs, fish and snakes. Priests would choose the right type and colour of animal that was best for the sacrifice.

### FACT

Important gods had wider reign over war, the sea, harvests and so on. And to make things even more complicated, the Romans adopted gods from other nations, especially those nations whose soldiers showed courage in fighting.

# BAD THINGS HAPPEN

## SATURNALIA

This festival, held in mid-December to honour the god Saturn, was a time of merriment and role reversal. The man of the house – the master normally – might be called to prepare a feast for the slaves. He and his sons would also serve the meal – and their 'guests' could be very, very demanding!

### FACT

Many people believe that the 'merriness' of a merry Christmas dates back to the Roman celebration of Saturnalia, which was also in December.

### FACT

Often the sacrificed animal was cooked as part of the ceremony. People would then share the cooked meat as part of the ritual.

# INSIDE KNOWLEDGE

## NO DAY OF REST?

The Romans originally used an eight-day 'market week' but things changed soon after Julius Caesar's reign began. Rome adopted the seven-day week that we now use. Certain days were set aside for legal functions, whilst other days became public holidays.

## FACT

The Romans also noted three special days in each month based on the three phases of the Moon. The day of the new Moon was 'kalends' (like our word 'calendar'), the day of the first quarter Moon was 'nones' and the day of the full Moon was 'ides'.

# A ROMAN WORK DAY

I have had to learn a great deal about my father's work. And the best way to do this has been by watching him closely. As a member of the Senate, my father attends sessions full of fancy speeches about politics and history. Writing and delivering such speeches, a skill called oratory, is something that I have to learn in grammar school.

JULIUS CAESAR WAS STABBED TO DEATH IN THE SENATE ON THE IDES OF MARCH.

# BAD THINGS HAPPEN

## ONE FOR THE ROAD

Roman workers, like their modern counterparts, often stopped for a drink on the way home. But good cheer could lead to violence and robbery if these drinkers weren't careful – they had to find their way home through dark alleys.

### FACT

Roman taverns weren't just for drinking. Many of them had ovens for baking bread and charcoal fires for cooking meat and fish.

### FACT

By the time that Rome stopped being a republic and became an empire, the Senate had lost most of its power. Senators still made speeches and discussed important issues, but only the Emperor had real power.

# INSIDE KNOWLEDGE

## FACT

Pompeii was covered in a blanket of ash and lava when Mt Vesuvius erupted in AD 79. Peeling away that blanket has revealed much of the city, and helped historians learn much more about Roman life.

## ROMAN PETS

Cats became popular pets in ancient Rome, thanks to the influence of Egyptians (who worshipped them as gods) and other Eastern nations. But the most popular pets for Roman boys were dogs. Sometimes they would take the dogs hunting, but children also loved to train dogs to fetch sticks, chase after balls or roll over – just as children play with dogs now.

# COULD YOU WIN A SWORDFIGHT?

Our family has spent a few days visiting relatives and sightseeing in Pompeii, one of the towns south of Rome. Pompeii is beside the sea and stands at the edge of a beautiful bay. Looming over the bay is the towering Mount Vesuvius, a volcano that sometimes groans and sends smoke rising out from its peak.

MY COUSIN LIVES IN POMPEII AND HE SAYS IT'S GREAT FUN TO GO EXPLORING NEAR VESUVIUS BUT THE VOLCANO'S GROANS CAN BE QUITE SCARY...

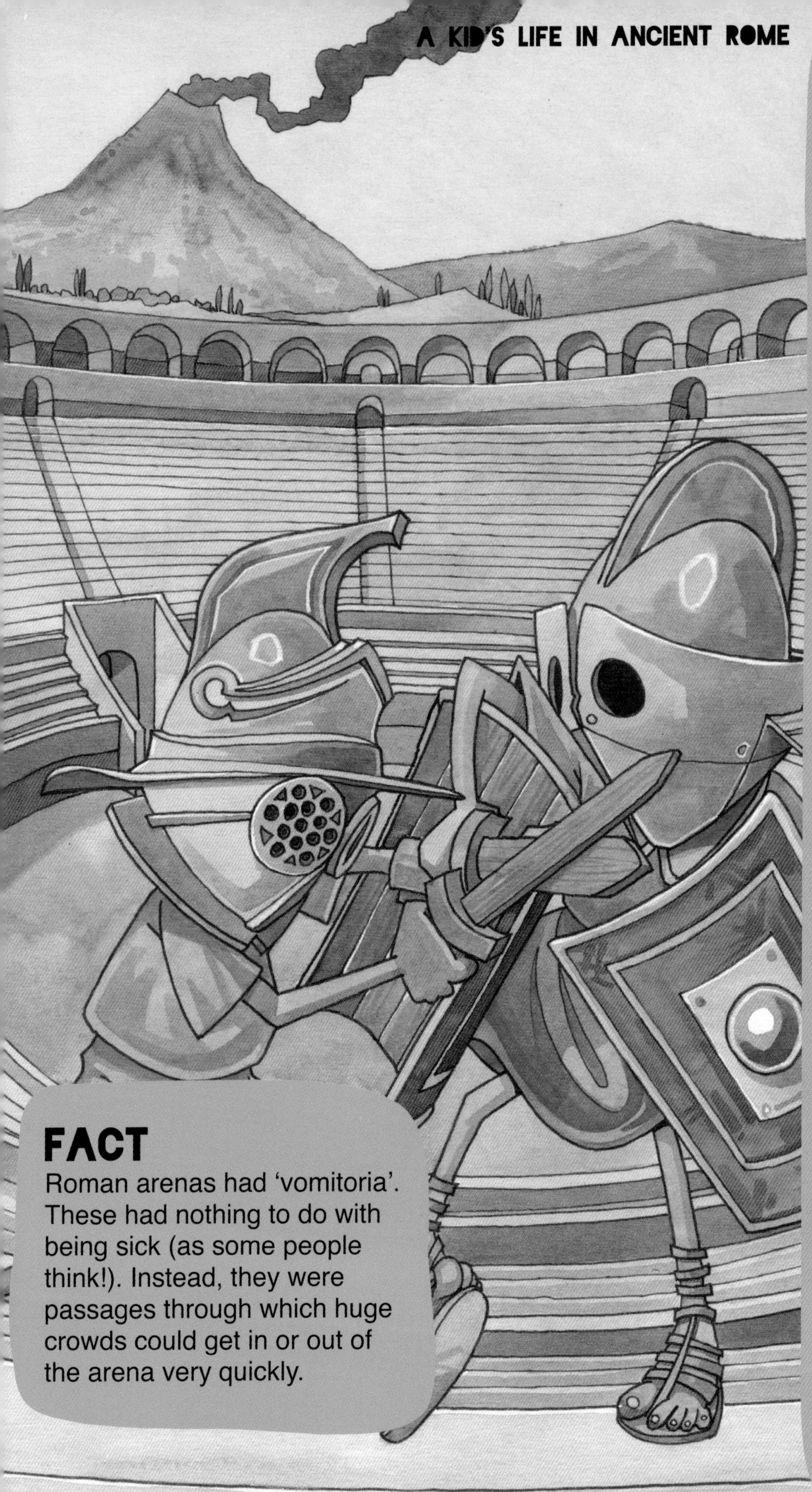

# BAD THINGS HAPPEN

## GLADIATORS

Roman boys loved to stage mock fights and battles. They weren't allowed to use real weapons but used sticks or wooden swords to copy the way gladiators fought. The most famous gladiator contests were in Rome's Colosseum, but Pompeii and other cities also had arenas where gladiators would fight, sometimes to the death.

## THE SMOKING FIELD

The sons of local farmers had less time to play. They were often hard at work in fields on the slopes below Vesuvius. Plants grow well in the soil because the ash acts like 'vitamins' to nourish any growth.

### FACT

Roman arenas had 'vomitoria'. These had nothing to do with being sick (as some people think!). Instead, they were passages through which huge crowds could get in or out of the arena very quickly.

# GLOSSARY

**anniculus** A Roman child's first birthday celebration.

**armour** Metal clothing worn by soldiers for protection.

**atrium** An open central court at the heart of a Roman house.

**bulla** A locket worn by young Roman boys to protect them from bad luck.

**catacombs** A huge network of caves outside the walls of Rome where Romans were buried.

**citizen** A person with full legal rights.

**clan** A wide family group, including distant relatives.

**Colosseum** The most famous arena in the Roman Empire, located in central Rome.

**compluvium** A space in the ceiling of the atrium that allowed rain to come through and collect below.

**dowry** Money or other types of wealth that a bride's family would offer to the husband at a wedding.

**Forum** A collection of government buildings and temples where Rome's most important business was conducted.

**Freedmen** Former slaves who had either bought their freedom or had it granted to them by their masters.

**garum** A strong-smelling sauce made from fermented fish guts used widely in Roman cooking.

**gymnasium** A club, like a modern scout group, where Roman boys would play sports and learn about being good citizens.

**ides** The name given to the day of a full Moon.

**insulae** The large blocks of flats in Rome and in other cities in the Empire.

**Julius Caesar** (100BC–44BC) A Roman military leader who gained political power, ending the Republic and establishing the Imperial era.

**kalends** The name given to the day of a new Moon.

**legion** A disciplined group of about 5,000 soldiers forming part of the overall Roman army.

**midwife** Someone (usually a woman) who delivers babies.

**nones** The name given to the first quarter Moon.

**paterfamilias** The 'father of the family', a name given to the husband (and master) of a Roman household.

**spongia** A sea sponge attached to a long stick and used in Roman public toilets.

# INDEX